CONTENTS

TURN YOUR HOUSE INTO A SCIENCE LAB!

Did you know that your toys can teach you about why things move the way they do? **Forces** push and pull things to make them stop and go. You can see forces in action everywhere – from space to the park to the playroom. Get ready to have some fun with forces and *motion*!

force any action that changes the movement of an object

motion movement

Safety first!

You may need an adult's help for some of these experiments. But most of them can be done on your own. If you have a question about how to do a step safely, make sure you ask an adult. Think safety first!

TURN TO PAGE 20 TO SEE HOW THE SCIENCE WORKS IN EACH EXPERIMENT!

MOVE IT!

Have you ever watched a racing car zoom by? Or have you spotted an aeroplane flying high up in the sky? These motions couldn't happen without forces. Check out a few ways to make your own toy car whiz forward!

Materials:

string

pencil

tape

toy car

Stay in motion

An object that's resting will stay still unless a force makes it move. An object that's moving will keep moving until a force makes it stop. This is Newton's First Law of Motion. Isaac Newton was a **scientist**. He lived from 1643 to 1727.

Steps:

1. Put a toy car on a flat surface. Use your finger to push it forward.

2. Push a pencil against the car to make the car go.

3. Use tape to attach a piece of string to the car. Pull the string to move the car.

4. Repeat steps 2 and 3 with the car turned upside down. Which way was easier? Can you think of other kinds of forces? How many ways can you move the car?

scientist person who studies the world around us

STOP THAT TRUCK!

When an object is moving, **frictional** forces can stop it. When you run along a pavement, you can stop because of the friction between your shoes and the ground. But what if you run along a pavement and want to stop in a puddle? Friction is still there, but there is less of it. Try playing with friction using some of your toys!

Materials:

toy truck

two building blocks

tape measure

friction force produced when two objects rub against each other; friction slows objects down

Steps:

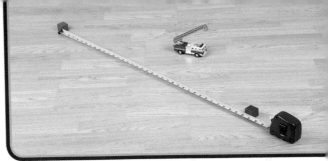

1. Sit on a flat, hard floor. Measure a distance of 1 metre (3 feet). Use blocks to mark the start and finish lines. ●·······

2. Push the truck so it rolls from the start to the finish. ●··········

3. Measure 1 metre (3 ft) outside in the grass. Use the blocks to mark the start and finish lines. ●·········

4. Push the truck so it rolls from the start to the finish. Was it harder to push the truck on the floor or the grass?

5. Try rolling the truck on a bumpy pavement or across gravel. Which surfaces have the most friction? ●············

Fact:
Rub your hands together quickly. You will feel how friction can also cause heat.

9

WHAT GOES UP MUST COME DOWN

Why does a ball fall to the ground after you've thrown it? Because **gravity** is at work. Gravity is a type of force that makes things fall to Earth. Catch gravity in action with this simple activity!

Materials:

a thick cardboard box, the bigger the better

scissors

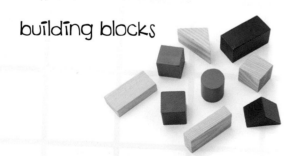

building blocks

a handful of small balls or marbles

gravity force that pulls objects with mass together; gravity pulls objects down towards the centre of Earth

Steps:

1. **With an adult's help, cut long strips out of a box. Bend the strips so the edges are curved slightly. These are your ramps.**

2. **Use blocks to set up the ramps. Some will be steeper than others.**

3. **Let balls or marbles roll down each ramp. Which direction do they roll in?**

4. **Release two balls at the same time on two ramps. Have a race! Which ball rolls faster? Why might that be?**

Fact:

Some planets have more gravity than others. Gravity affects how much things weigh. If you weigh 25 kilograms on Earth, you would weigh 63 kilograms on Jupiter. You would only weigh 10 kilograms on Mars. On the Sun, you would weigh 699 kilograms!

FIGHTING FORCES

Gravity pulls objects towards Earth. Big, tall buildings are built to resist gravity. Thick walls stop them falling down. Have a go at this experiment and think like a builder using some of your toys!

Materials:

interlocking toy bricks

Steps:

1. **Build a tower using interlocking toy bricks. How high can you make it before it tips over?** ●

2. **Try building a second tower with a thicker base. Build it higher than the first tower. Why can you build the second tower higher than the first?** ●

3. **Keep adding bricks to make your tower as tall as you can. Can you think of other tricks you can use to build a taller tower and resist the force of gravity?**

13

TUG AWAY

More force produces more motion. If you lightly tap a football, it won't move very far. But if you kick the ball hard, it will travel further. See for yourself in a game of tug-of-war. Prepare to pull as hard as you can!

Materials:

a friend or sibling

a rope or an old sheet twisted into a rope

an adult

Tip:
Ask an adult to supervise this activity.

Steps:

1. **Find a friend who is about the same size as you. Hold one end of the rope. Ask your friend to hold the other end. On the count of three, both of you should pull as hard as you can. Who won?**

2. **In the next match, use just one arm while your friend uses two arms. Try again using two arms while your friend uses only one. Did the results change? Who won the matches?**

3. **Now try playing against an adult. Did you win or lose?**

Weight matters

Mass is the amount of material in an object. A person who weighs more than you do, has more mass. An object with more mass needs more force to change its motion. Imagine running next to an adult. It would take more force to stop the adult than it would take for you to stop.

15

CRAZY BALLOONS

Large bin lorries move forwards. Skateboards can **curve** around a corner. Why do things move the way they do? In this activity, you can see how forces make objects move in all sorts of ways. Have a balloon race with a friend!

Materials:

a friend or sibling

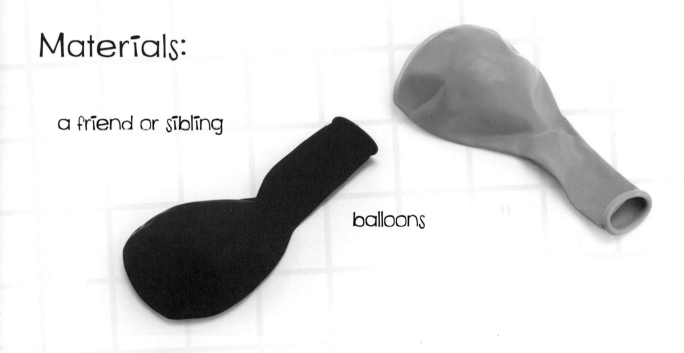

balloons

curve bend or turn gently and continuously

Steps:

1. Blow up a balloon. Ask your friend to do the same. Pinch the opening shut with your fingers.

2. Stand side-by-side with your friend, and let the balloons go. What happened to the balloons? Which balloon stayed in the air longer? Did they start by moving in the same direction?

3. Now face each other. Repeat Steps 1 and 2. Which way does each balloon fly? Did you notice that the balloon moved in the opposite direction to the direction of the air being released from the balloon?

Tip:

With more air, a balloon can fly further.

LEVER POWER

Machines often produce force. Some machines are large, such as tractors. Other machines are smaller and simpler. A simple machine can even be a screw holding up a picture frame on a wall in your house. Try creating force in this easy experiment with a simple machine!

Materials:

a ruler

triangle-shaped block

heavy objects, like a book or a rock

machine piece of equipment that is used to do a job or make it easier to do something

Steps:

1. Place a ruler on a block like a see-saw to make a *lever*.

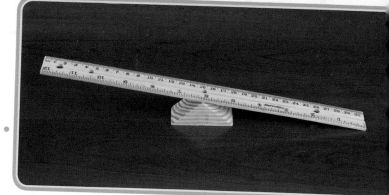

2. Put a heavy object on one end of the lever. Push down on the other end.

3. Experiment by moving the block to change the position of the lever. How could you build a lever to lift a heavier weight? Could you make a lever strong enough to lift a person?

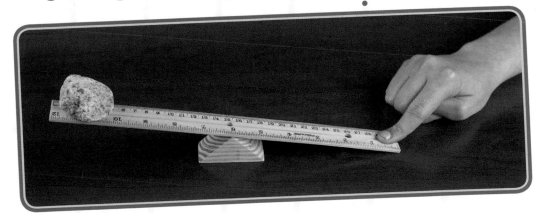

lever bar that turns on a resting point and is used to lift items

WHY IT WORKS

Would you like to know how these amazing experiments work? Here is the science behind the fun!

PAGE 6 - MOVE IT!

To move a toy, you could push or pull it. You could blow it, drop it or kick it. There are many possible forces that can act on a toy or object.

PAGE 8 - STOP THAT TRUCK!

There is more friction on rough surfaces than on smooth surfaces. On a smooth surface, the truck moves easily. Outside, the grass rubs against the truck wheels, slowing the truck down. A truck pushed with the same force will move further on a smooth floor than on soil or grass.

PAGE 10 - WHAT GOES UP MUST COME DOWN

Gravity stops the air around us and other objects floating off into space. Gravity also makes objects fall to the ground. This pull is why the balls or marbles roll down the ramps. If the objects are the same size and mass, and the ramps are the same height, the balls will roll down the ramp at the same speed.

PAGE 12 - FIGHTING FORCES

Tall buildings need to be built correctly. Otherwise, gravity will pull them down! With a thicker base, the building is more *stable*, like the tower you built.

PAGE 14 - TUG AWAY

A person with more mass will usually be able to produce more force. Compared to a child, a big adult will be able to pull harder and will probably win a game of tug-of-war.

PAGE 16 - CRAZY BALLOONS

When you let go of a balloon, look at which way the air is blowing out of it. The balloon will move in the opposite direction. Putting more air in the balloon will make it fly through the air for longer.

PAGE 18 - LEVER POWER

People have been using levers for thousands of years. Even your arm is a sort of lever! Less force is needed to lift something when a lever is used than when a lever isn't used. Levers and other types of machine make work easier for people.

stable not easily moved

GLOSSARY

curve bend or turn gently and continuously

force any action that changes the movement of an object

friction force produced when two objects rub against each other; friction slows objects down

gravity force that pulls objects with mass together; gravity pulls objects down towards the centre of Earth

lever bar that turns on a resting point and is used to lift items

machine piece of equipment that is used to do a job or make it easier to do something

mass amount of material in an object

motion movement

scientist person who studies the world around us

stable not easily moved

READ MORE

Levers (How Toys Work), Sian Smith (Raintree, 2012)

Machines on a Construction Site (Machines at Work), Sian Smith (Raintree, 2014)

Making Machines with Levers (Simple Machine Projects), Chris Oxlade (Raintree, 2015)

Super Cool Forces and Motion Activities with Max Axiom (Max Axiom Science and Engineering Activities), Agnieszka Biskup (Raintree, 2015)

WEBSITES

www.bbc.co.uk/bitesize/ks2/science/physical_processes/
Use your knowledge of forces and mass to help win a gymnastics competition!

www.kidsdiscover.com/spotlight/force-motion-kids/
Discover fascinating facts about forces and motion and take a look at some amazing photographs that show forces in action in the world around us.

INDEX